A PATRON-CENTERED GUIDE

PUTTING *Service* INTO LIBRARY STAFF TRAINING

JOANNE M. BESSLER

LAMA Occasional Papers Series

American Library Association
Chicago and London 1994

Editorial manager: Joan A. Grygel

Cover design by Megan DeSantis/ALA Marketing

Interior design by Donavan Vicha

Composition by ALA Production Services in Souvenir and Optima using Ventura Publisher 3.0. Camera-ready pages output on a Varityper VT600 laser printer.

Printed on 50-pound Glatfelter, a pH-neutral stock, and bound in 10-point C1S cover stock by McNaughton & Gunn.

The paper used in this publication meets the minimum requirements of American National Standard for Information Sciences—Permanence of Paper for Printed Library Materials, ANSI Z39.48-1984. ∞

Library of Congress Cataloging-in-Publication Data

Bessler, Joanne M.
    Putting "service" into library staff training : a library
manager's training guide / Joanne M. Bessler.
       p. cm. —(Occasional papers / Library Administration and
Management Association)
    Includes bibliographical references and index.
    ISBN 0-8389-3437-4
    1. Library employees—Training of—United States. 2. Libraries
and readers—United States. 3. Library education (Continuing
education)—United States. 4. Library personnel management—
United States. I. Title. II. Series: Occasional papers (Library
Administration and Management Association)
Z668.5.B48 1994
023'.8'0973—dc20   93-31055

Printed in the United States of America.

98 97 96 95 94   5 4 3 2 1

Contents

Preface

THIS GUIDE IS DESIGNED to help library managers teach staff at all levels and in every area of library work (public services, technical services, or administrative services) the attitudes and skills that will make their library a service-oriented organization. The principles offered here apply to an endless array of settings and situations. The anticipated audience includes library deans and directors, assistant directors, department heads, and unit managers in public, academic, special, state, and school libraries.

Due to the breadth and variety of audience needs, this guide offers some suggestions that are valid for some groups of readers and not for others. Although the case studies and examples will represent various levels of management and types of library settings, they will not cover every possible configuration. Each chapter ends with a brief "Planning Aid" that suggests some initial steps for turning the chapter's message into action.

Throughout this guide, all of the managers and patrons are described as female and all of the line employees and trainees as male. This assumption is based on no known model, but on the desire to avoid pronoun problems.

This guide uses the terms *patron, customer, library user,* and *client* interchangeably. No one term seems universally accepted by staff in all different types of libraries and service organizations. Although this guide addresses a broad audience with differing interests, two concepts remain consistent: *you* always refers to you the reader, and improving service is always the goal.

Introduction

THIS GUIDE MIGHT BEST be described as a library service training and survival manual. It builds on the training literature of librarianship and customer-service training research from a variety of professions. It encourages managers to identify and describe their service ideals, to transform these ideals into realistic goals, and to guide both new and experienced staff in fulfilling these ideals, even in the face of adversity.

Faced with overworked and strained staff, ever-growing and competing patron expectations, technological turmoil, and shrinking budget allocations, today's library managers may hesitate to increase their commitment to training. Yet it is these very demands that make such a commitment critical.

No library can be all things to all people. This guide encourages library managers to focus their staff's energy on the services most prized by their own patrons. Once they have clarified their library's service priorities, they can present them in every aspect of training. This will attune the staff member's every action, every policy interpretation, and every choice in priorities to the needs of his own institution.

Service-focused training will also give managers and staff common-core principles to guide them during an era of turbulent

1

change. As technology revolutionizes what is possible and as a changing user group expresses radically new demands, old policies, procedures, and dictums will sink into obsolescence. Yesterday's policies will not guide staff effectively. Staff will need to understand their library's renewed goals and be trained to put them into action.

Although many sources are quoted in this guide, one book, *In Search of Excellence: Lessons from America's Best Run Companies,* must be given primary honor, for it popularized the service revolution in the United States. Four observations made by its authors, Tom J. Peters and Robert H. Waterman, Jr., should be hung near every library manager's desk. That is, excellent companies

> fawn on their customers;
>
> listen to their employees, and treat them like adults;
>
> allow their innovative product and service "champions" long tethers;
>
> allow some chaos in return for quick action and regular experimentation.

CHAPTER ONE

Getting an Image: Developing a Mission Statement

TO EXCEL AS A SERVICE ORGANIZATION, a library must create an identity as a service. Developing a formal mission statement is a critical first step in this process of self-discovery. Although it is best for this step to be part of a larger, institutional strategic-planning process, it need not be. A meaningful library or departmental mission statement can be developed with proper consultation. The appendix offers some sample mission statements.

Writing a mission statement is a time-consuming task. It is a bit like psychoanalysis: the organization examines who it is, how it became the way it is, and what it wants to be in the future. As arduous as this step is, it must be done to give your library's administrators, funders, staff, and patrons a common perception about what your library is supposed to do.

Whether you are designing a mission statement for an entire library or for a single department, the most important rule in drafting a mission statement is to share the experience. This is not the time for a discourse on your personal beliefs about librarianship. Your library needs a mission statement that (a) reflects your organization's goals and values, (b) expresses reality as well as idealism, and (c) reflects values that your staff embrace.

To write a successful and practical mission statement, you must begin with point c. Although your library wasn't created for the benefit of the staff, the quality of your service depends upon their commitment. Before you gather and refine input from your organization's administrators, funders, and patrons, you must talk to your staff. Give them the opportunity and time to read articles about service and to watch videos offering example experiences at banks, restaurants, hotels, etc.

As staff members become more aware of service issues, encourage them to document their impressions about patron needs. Ask staff to suggest ways to gather patron and administrative input, and include all levels of staff in gathering and analyzing user suggestions. Although some will resist philosophical discussions on service values, most staff will support a mission that they have helped create.

What Do Customers Want?

The primary principle cited in service literature is "Find Out What the Customer Wants." A library's customers include its funders and administrators as well as its patrons (FAP). For a public library, this group might consist of a board of directors, members of the local government, and citizens of all ages, interests, and abilities. For a state library, the customer base might include government officials, libraries throughout the state, and various citizen groups. Each library must identify its own FAP and incorporate their values into its mission statement.

Some libraries have sharply defined responsibilities. For example, special libraries with very focused user needs usually are expected to provide fast, accurate, and up-to-date information tailored to the specific needs of the clientele. Libraries serving large and diverse groups, however, often have murkier mandates. Clarifying customer expectations for your library is the most demanding part of developing a mission statement. To gain a comprehensive understanding of these needs, you (and a large percentage of your staff) will have to combine a number of approaches. Six sample approaches follow.

1. *Gather historical information.*

   Collect and analyze existing documents and data that describe your community, its composition and identity, and what it historically has wanted from your library. Such administrative artifacts as existing mission and policy statements, annual reports, college bulletins, etc., will reveal what has been expected of your library in the past.

2. *Interview key FAP.*

   Armed with information about the history of your organization, meet with key funders, administrators, and internal and external patrons to determine current needs and expectations.

3. *Create an issue board.*

   Use display space with materials that allow self-posting of responses to invite informal patron input in defining your library's mission. Although you will gather dozens of repetitive or even silly ideas, you will gain a few unique ideas from your users' perspectives. You will also identify those issues that attract a great deal of interest.

4. *Invite FAP to participate in a focus group.*

   As you identify individuals who are genuinely interested in your library, build one or more focus groups to discuss specific issues and challenges relating to your library's mission. To attract a representative group you may need to offer some modest incentive, such as a free lunch or some honor at a Friends of the Library celebration.

5. *Study the goals and funding patterns of your funders, administrators, and patrons.*

   City and county governments, school boards, legislators, and trustees all tend to put their money where their mission is. Watch your organization's budget. What type of requests are being funded? What justifications appeal to the administrators? If your city or county government is focused on fighting juvenile crime, the library might focus attention on programming for restless youths. If your company is exploring foreign markets, you may want to highlight international databases.

6. *Listen while you play.*

If you socialize with any FAP, keep your ears open. Are they looking for information or services that the library does or could supply? Individuals who have no patience for reading your memos or surveys and who feel far too busy for any formal presentations or lectures can be reached by a casual comment or sounded out informally.

What Can You Promise to Deliver?

Libraries teem with endless potential but are bound by finite resources. The FAP in your life will most likely identify far more needs than you can possibly handle. Worse yet, many libraries serve patron groups who hold different dreams about ideal service. Stretching to meet all of these needs can doom your library to mediocrity, your staff to exhaustion, and you to extinction. You must organize the needs and expectations of your clientele into some kind of master vision. That vision must reflect most closely the dreams of the power holders in your user community, and it must be attainable. Once you and your staff have identified the vision your funders, administrators, and patrons have for your library, you can formulate it into a clear statement. You must then take this statement back to your FAP for review. The FAP must understand the costs, options, and choices associated with the mission and be prepared to pay these costs or to modify the mission.

Commit your library to excellence in one area of high interest to your administration or community. In his book, *Client-Centered Service: How to Keep Them Coming Back for More,* David W. Cottle describes this commitment as defining "what you want to be famous for."[1]

In the business world, corporations define themselves with snappy phrases—"when it absolutely, positively has to be there overnight" (Federal Express Corporation); "quality is job 1" (Ford Motor Company); "we try harder" (Avis automobile rentals); and "you can count on Sears" (Sears Roebuck & Company). Although your library will strive to excel in a large number of areas, you can generate broad support by highlighting one special achievement

---

1. David W. Cottle, *Client-Centered Service: How to Keep Them Coming Back for More* (New York: John Wiley & Sons, 1990), 67.

that differentiates your library from all other libraries and links you to your organization's highest goals.

Your Philosophy of Service

An effective mission statement describes your library's commitments in terms of what your patrons want and what you can deliver. The statement should also describe your philosophy of service. What approach will your library use in delivering its services? How will your users be treated? You may want to underscore your commitment to user education, to providing free and equal access to information, or to providing individualized services designed to meet the special needs of each user.

The "philosophy of service" section of the mission statement may indicate the organization's approach to policies. Although it will not list individual rules, it might say that "policies are guidelines meant to be interpreted to enhance service" or that "careful adherence to policies guarantees the most service for the most people most of the time."

Planning Aid

Identify three ways in which you could involve appropriate staff in your library or department in answering the following questions:

- Why does this library exist?
- What is distinctive about the community we serve?
- What do the FAP want from us?
- What do we want to be special or unique about our library services? What do we want to be famous for?
- How will this library be different in five years? in ten years?

CHAPTER TWO

Recruiting Kindred Spirits

T O INFLUENCE SERVICE, a mission statement must touch people, policies, and procedures. Involving your staff in creating and interpreting your library's mission can promote internal support for that mission. A vacant or new position, however, offers you the opportunity to hire people who have been attracted by the principles of your unique mission. To capitalize on any recruiting opportunities that good fortune may offer, make your library's vision of service evident in every phase of the search process.

Designing the Position

Start out by defining every job to be filled as a *service* position. Make certain that every position description in your library mentions your patrons, highlights the individual's service responsibilities, and allocates time for these activities. For instance, the job description for a cataloger might specify that the cataloger will meet monthly with the reference staff to discuss patron difficulties in searching the catalog and options for reducing errors.

Within the job description and in the official job posting, you must identify necessary qualifications. The routine phrase "works well with people" will not discourage misanthropes from applying nor will it lure the "best and the brightest." To attract people who are genuinely interested in service, underscore service in your documentation using phrases such as

- Technical skills are highly desirable, but the ability to listen to and accommodate the differing needs of our patrons is crucial.
- Assignments will vary in accordance with the needs of our patrons.
- Applicants must possess the ability to deal with changing priorities based on patron needs.
- Preference will be given to applicants who have developed and implemented programs to enhance patron services.
- We are seeking an individual who can present the library as an exciting, fun, and valuable place for students to visit.
- Applicants must demonstrate respect and concern for patrons of all ages, races, and nationalities.
- Applicants must enjoy working with people and finding solutions to their library-related problems.

Sending the Right Message

A carefully phrased job description and posting may attract some excellent applicants. To find and win the best match for your library, show your service philosophy in every stage of the search process—from the first correspondence to the letter of welcome.

Your service ideals should be evident in your words and in your actions. You can stress your service commitment by

mentioning service in your initial letter to each applicant;

asking questions highlighting service: the individual's past contributions to service, his own philosophy of service, his techniques in handling patrons with unique needs, and his attitude toward rules;

giving the applicant your library's written mission statement.

The final way to show the applicant your library's concept of good service is by your and your staff's example. Treat each applicant as you want him to treat your patrons. From the initial review of the applications to the final selection of the employee, treat each individual with openness and respect. When putting into practice the legal imperatives of affirmative action, the Equal Employment Opportunity Act of 1972, and the Americans with Disabilities Act of 1990, go beyond the letter of the law. Use these laws to remind yourself and your staff that superb service staff do not come from a single mold.

Once you have selected the candidates for an interview, begin to woo them. Make your letters personable and informative. Offer each candidate as much assistance as possible in making travel arrangements. Throughout the interview, make certain that each candidate has the information and time he needs to evaluate the position. Look for opportunities to make your interview stand out in a candidate's mind as a delightful and stimulating experience.

Recognizing the Stars

The interview is a critical moment in time. During these hours or days, you must gain an in-depth understanding of the candidate and the candidate must get to know you. You must be primed for the day. In planning the schedule and drafting the interview questions, prepare yourself to do the following:

- Listen to the candidate's choice of topics and descriptions of situations. Is service mentioned? Are the patrons portrayed in a sympathetic manner?
- Note the candidate's own listening skills.
- Pay attention to your own reaction to the candidate. Although you must guard against certain prejudices (such as preferring to hire people who dress or talk as you do), you should notice if you feel annoyed with the candidate's tone or bored by long-winded answers.
- Watch how the candidate treats the secretaries and individuals who are not involved in the interview process.

The final (and absolutely essential) quality to watch for in hiring a service-oriented individual is the demonstrated ability to do the job. You must not become so enthralled with the interpersonal skills of an applicant that you overlook a lack of knowledge and experience. To give quality service the individual must be skilled at the job he is hired to perform. Evidence of potential is needed for entry-level positions.

Working with the Unsolicited Recruit

At times organizational or labor rules can limit your ability to recruit candidates and select new staff. Your new employee may arrive by reassignment. Both you and the new employee may view the move with something less than delight. As a manager, however, you must use whatever freedom you have to make this a good match.

A job change offers an employee the opportunity to redefine himself. A new position provides the experienced employee with a chance to learn new skills and to abandon old behaviors. Encourage your staff member to make the most of this opportunity. Spend time listening to the employee's goals and concerns. Through listening and coaching, help the reassigned staff member build service ideals into his new self-image.

Planning Aid

Look at one current job description in your library and rewrite it to reflect service in the

description of responsibilities;

choice of vocabulary;

qualifications and skills desired.

CHAPTER THREE

Orienting toward Service

I T IS EASY TO TALK about one's "philosophy of service" in the generally congenial setting of an interview when interview participants are isolated from the hubbub of daily activity. On Day 1, however, most new employees get a glimpse of the real library atmosphere. Deadlines, ringing phones, quirky computers, and harried staff replace philosophical and theoretical musings. The manager's role is to make certain that the "philosophy of service" is highlighted throughout the orientation process.

Research shows that "employees form long-lasting impressions of the organization within the first 60–90 days on the job."[1] To highlight the library's commitment to excellent service and to make the orientation process an effective service boost, you must make certain that your program says that service is important, shows that service is important, and treats the new employee in a service-oriented way.

---

1. Pamela A. Kaul, "First Impressions Last (Effective Orientation Programs)," *Association Management* 41 (May 1989): 18, 29–31.

Talk about Service

When you are training a new employee, restate your library's commitment to service. Say it a dozen ways. Review the library's formal mission statement with the new employee and describe how it applies to the individual's unit and to the individual's specific job responsibilities. Give the employee a copy of the mission statement and offer him a list of basic concepts that serve as a touchstone for future independent decision making. For example, guidelines from the University of Notre Dame Libraries state:

1. Our patrons' needs should be the focus of all of our efforts. Each person's job is to consider and care about our patrons' needs.

2. Our goal is to offer the maximum amount of service feasible at a given point in time.

3. To best use our finite resources, service priorities must be set.

4. Quality service depends upon the judgment, imagination, and responsiveness of individual staff. Supervisors must sensitize their staff to the broad range of requests and special service needs which can be presented by patrons and should prepare their staff to respond to these requests in a positive, helpful manner.

5. Our patrons include current members of the Notre Dame community, future generations of that community, and members of the scholarly community at large. While immediate needs often demand our attention, we must consider future patrons in planning our development and in building and preserving our collections.

6. Our staff are patrons too. We must show each other the same respect and helpfulness that we show our patrons.[2]

Prepare Staff to Give Quality Service

If you want the employee to value service, treat training as a worthwhile process. Use some of your *time* (that rare and precious

---

2. Robert C. Miller, *Working in the Libraries.* (Unpublished paper, University of Notre Dame Libraries, 1990), 4.

commodity) to teach staff your expectations. Commit some real dollars to training. The average American company spends an amount equal to approximately 1.7 percent of its annual salary budget for training and development.

In their outstanding book, *The Service Edge,* Ron Zemke and Dick Schaaf report that America's top service companies make a major investment in training. Service leaders such as Disneyland, Procter and Gamble, L.L. Bean, and McDonald's insist that new staff receive weeks of extensive orientation and instruction. For instance, Zemke and Schaaf report that a new product hotline representative at Procter and Gamble must spend six weeks training before answering a single call.[3] This attention to preparation for serving clients reflects the importance of clients to the organization.

In a for-profit organization, a happy customer equals profits. Training staff to offer quality service can boost a corporation's income. With this prospect in mind, American companies now devote approximately $45 billion dollars a year to training and staff development.[4] For a nonprofit organization, a happy customer is equally important. Pleasing customers can improve public relations and increase support for the library. Even more importantly, satisfying customers can improve staff satisfaction and library effectiveness. As customer complaints decrease, staff will have more time to spend on the productive and positive aspects of their jobs.

To guarantee that your staff are primed to give service when they are put on the line, develop and use a systematic training outline. Design your outline to stress the need for achievement in

reflecting your library's service ideals;

skillfully performing the job responsibilities;

cooperating with other staff to upgrade service.

Figure 1 offers a sample outline that suggests potential goals for each of the training categories for the first four months of training. This outline is designed for a staff member in a university library reference department. The elements selected should reflect the needs of your specific department or library.

---

3. Ron Zemke with Dick Schaaf, *The Service Edge: 101 Companies That Profit from Customer Care* (New York: New American Library, 1989), 335.

4. Ron Zemke, "Training in Campaign '92," *Training* 29 (Oct. 1992), 69.

Figure 1. Library Orientation Outline

Organizational Values

FIRST WEEK	FIRST MONTH	FOURTH MONTH
Institution's mission Library's mission Individual's role in mission Relationship between mission and evaluations and budget priorities	Library's approach to rules Departmental rules that may frustrate patrons Goals behind key policies	How and when to bend rules Problem solvers in other units How and when to gather patron concerns and suggestions and what to do with them

General Orientation

FIRST WEEK	FIRST MONTH	FOURTH MONTH
Location of primary resources and services Basic desk procedures Library hours Emergency procedures	How to operate equipment How to complete necessary forms Phone system tricks Locations of smaller library units	The sequence of processing orders Directions to popular locations on campus or in the city The importance of continuing education and the types of programs that are available

Reference

FIRST WEEK	FIRST MONTH	FOURTH MONTH
How to do simple searches in the catalog Types of reference sources Analyzing reference questions Location of the most frequently requested sources	How to do complicated keyword searches Desk reference collection How to use primary indexes How to use the sources in one popular academic subject area, such as education, that has "user friendly" reference sources	How to use the more-complex sources in various academic disciplines and special collections, such as government documents, business, and law How to tap informational resources that extend beyond the local collection by using sources such as OCLC, the Internet, or online table of contents services

Interpersonal Skills

FIRST WEEK	FIRST MONTH	FOURTH MONTH
Greeting patrons Encouraging patron follow-up Phone techniques Treating staff as patrons	Listening skills Making referrals Receiving referrals Coping with stressful individuals and situations	Dealing with irate patrons Saying "no" Dealing with patrons with special needs Intervening when another staff member is misinforming a patron

The sources listed in the Bibliography at the end of this guide are packed with ideas and case studies that can strengthen your training program. The following are three of the most valuable.

The *Handbook of Library Training Practice* by Ray Prytherch (1986) is a two-volume work that includes chapters on topics such as handling users, customer care, assertiveness training, and training for library work in multicultural Britain. Chapters include case studies, self-tests, and sources for training videos, films, etc.

The National Institute of Business Management's *Service and Satisfaction: A Frontline Employee's Workbook* (1989) offers well-focused chapters on dealing with customers of all types. Chapters cover topics such as making a good first impression, the art of listening, and negotiating with customers.

The *BBP Customer Service Management Handbook* from the Bureau of Better Business Practice (1987) includes excellent chapters on all areas affecting service. Chapter Five, "Training for Superior Service," provides a series of suggestions on choosing and using the most appropriate training methods.

A well-prepared trainer armed with a solid training program can help staff start out right. However, keep in mind that "actual life in your company is the real trainer. The way the frontline people and their supervisors act, the kind of performance that gets rewarded, the day-to-day attitudes that the workers have toward each other and toward customers—these are what your people will learn and practice."[5]

Offer Model Service

Treat the new employee-in-training kindly. Staff should be treated as considerately as you treat your patrons. Chapter Five describes model behavior to use when interacting with a patron. This style should be normal and natural in welcoming new employees as

---

5. Clay Carr, *Frontline Customer Service: 15 Keys to Customer Satisfaction* (New York: John Wiley & Sons, 1990), 84.

well. During the orientation period, your primary goal should be to model the behavior you want to see.

Greet the new employee with enthusiasm. Although you may be working with a structured training outline, make certain that you are attuned to the individual employee. Take time to find out about the employee. Listen for and adjust to individual needs. Introduce the new staff member to other staff and involve other staff in welcoming the new person. Encourage staff to serve as "coaches" for new staff—teaching new employees the best ways to handle service challenges. Although you will never win every employee to your service philosophy, you can arouse some interest, thoughtfulness, and support by involving your staff in training others.

Planning Aid

A critical part of orientation training is showing staff who do not work at a service desk how their work affects patrons. To help you prepare this part of your orientation program, ask staff to develop examples demonstrating how specific tasks affect service. For example, the process of binding serials is filled with decisions and actions that have an impact upon service. Staff might list service considerations such as: How does the timing of binding affect current and future patrons? How do errors in bindery records disrupt service and exhaust funds? Although you may not have time to list the service implications of every job in your library, your supervisors need to know these ramifications in order to make "service" a real factor in training.

CHAPTER FOUR

Training the Trained: Training Experienced Staff to Focus on Service

MOST MANAGEMENT POSITIONS come with established staff in place. Sometimes these employees have been functioning in their areas for decades prior to your arrival or the beginning of the service initiative. Some have advanced degrees in library science or in other academic disciplines, and all have passed through what they view as their period of basic training. Although these staff may enthusiastically help build a training program with the intent of assisting newcomers, they may not understand or agree with the importance of similar training for experienced staff. If, however, you want your existing library staff to intensify their focus on service, you must attract the attention of all your staff, tie the training program to staff values, and reward staff participation.

Put the Spotlight on Your Staff

Start your discussions about service needs by focusing attention on your staff. Whether you are a library director or a unit manager, give your staff the attention that you want them to give patrons. Ask them to tell you their concerns and respond to these concerns whether or not they have a direct impact on service. At first, staff may focus on their personal work-related needs. Instead of pushing staff ahead into discussions about service, pause and listen. What issues or processes are frustrating staff? What do they value? What "services" can you offer staff?

You may not have a great deal of control over some of the most critical concerns. Budget realities, labor laws, and mandated policies from the administration may make it impossible for you to increase salaries, expand health benefits, or remodel facilities. You should, however, offer staff an opportunity to voice these crucial concerns. You should also provide them with any information that might increase staff awareness of long-term organizational pressures and constraints.

Fortunately, other concerns can be addressed by changing priorities or reallocating your own time. Even an impoverished manager at the lowest level of responsibility can meet requests to "improve communications" and "recognize good performance."

The manager will never be able to meet all staff needs. Staff, however, are not looking for miracles. Most staff will appreciate a manager who tries to meet some needs and who recognizes the many pressures faced by staff. Employees who know that their manager listens to their needs are more prepared to listen to and address the needs of their patrons.

Tie the Training to Staff Values

Although this guide focuses on service skills, your training program should cover technical skills as well as service strategies. Offering instructional sessions on new technologies and systems is a crucial contribution to quality service. Staff need to know how to do all aspects of their jobs well, not just how to relate to patrons. Furthermore staff are often more receptive to technical training than to presentations on interpersonal skills.

To increase receptivity to the service training sessions, make many of these sessions focus on commonly perceived problems. This should attract the attention and participation of experienced staff who have struggled with these very problems. Individuals who have dealt with irate individuals, speakers of other languages, and inarticulate patrons can usually be persuaded to attend skill-based training sessions that promise some assistance for coping with these experiences. Basing your training on common problems will also help you prepare new staff for the difficult situations that are most likely to occur in your specific library or department.

Although experienced staff are likely to be interested in the sessions that focus on their specific concerns, they may not be willing to make the commitment to more-general sessions. Think carefully before mandating attendance. The best participation may be indirect. Staff will gain more by participating in planning and teaching than by any form of forced participation.

If you feel that certain staff have mastered basic areas such as "telephone etiquette" and "greeting patrons," use their expertise to train new employees. Ask your experienced staff to review relevant videos or training materials and to suggest problem scenarios and model responses that might be used in your training program. Involving your staff in the development of the basic training program will enable them to review service principles and to share their own insights into successful service practices.

Reward Training Session Attendance

The primary reward that a staff member should get for attending any workshop or training session is self-satisfaction. No certificate of achievement, free lunch, or pat on the back will count as much as the employee's own recognition that the session was worth the time.

To achieve this degree of success, managers must craft sessions that are

informative, well-organized, and engaging;

focused on issues/needs that are important to the staff, such as dealing with stress during very busy periods or coping with endless changes in policies;

offered by individuals who possess evident expertise and credible credentials.

Satisfied trainees will help market future sessions.

Although intrinsic rewards are the greatest recompense for attending training sessions, compensation of other types can be encouraging. Note attendance on performance reviews and encourage the staff member to list it on his resume or on applications for internal promotions. You might also use personal notes to express appreciation for attendance and to invite suggestions for future sessions. Sessions might be grouped together as a series; anyone who completes the series might be given a certificate for his file or might be honored at an employee recognition day. Unless your organization is bound by restrictive regulations, you might be able to entice apathetic staff with the attraction of a box lunch or an afternoon retreat at an interesting location so they can discuss service demands in a relaxed and pleasant setting.

Work with Staff Who Resist Training Sessions

Some staff, however, will not attend voluntarily or keep an open mind to the principles presented. Some may sigh "people must accept me the way I am" or "I am too professional for smile lessons," etc. There is no foolproof way of responding to these statements. If the individual is adept in dealing with patrons and simply resents drains on his time, it might be best just to assign him to cover the unit so others can attend training sessions. If the individual is a true misanthrope who snarls and snaps at patrons, staff, and supervisors, no workshop will cause him to change his behavior. The lesson to teach this individual is that disservice will not be tolerated. On a one-to-one basis and in an ongoing manner, the manager must confront and correct the employee when he acts in a problematic way. The correction should be done in a private setting as promptly as possible. During this discussion, the manager should stress the importance placed on a service-oriented attitude and the consequences of continued performance problems in this area. The staff member must know his performance review will include a qualitative evaluation of his interpersonal skills and their effect on service. He should also know that ongoing problems in the area of service will lead to appropriate disciplinary action such as a salary freeze, a reassignment to a less attractive position, or dismissal. It is essential to deal promptly and decisively with this individual.

Planning Aid

Organize a service-planning day for your entire library, library system, or for a group of small local libraries. As a part of the program, organize two skits: one demonstrating ideal service as envisioned by your mission statement; the other portraying actual service in a system filled with inadequate resources, overworked and poorly prepared staff, and fickle technology. Ask staff to identify training activities that can help the library move from the present to the ideal.

CHAPTER FIVE

Defining Your Library's Service Commitments

T O OFFER DISTINCTIVE SERVICE requires more than desire. A clear target and technique are as essential as motivation. Every part-time worker, staff member, librarian, and administrator should know how to translate customer expectations about quality service and the library's service convictions into actions.

To help your staff respond well to patrons, use the training period to describe good service, provide a service role model, and give the staff members an opportunity to practice quality service in a nonthreatening situation. Chapters Five through Nine focus on specific training goals for instilling a service orientation in staff. This chapter will begin with the basics: greeting the patron, identifying the need, responding to the need, and following up.

Greeting the Patron

The patron is *IT*—the *I*ndividual *T*arget for your service skills. Whether the patron is a bank president requesting research assistance, a staff member dropping by to ask for a day off, or a second grader searching for a picture of Tyrannosaurus Rex, that patron must become the center of attention. Each individual contact represents what Karl Albrecht and Ron Zemke call the "Moment of Truth."[1] Staff training should encourage staff to focus on this moment.

Describing a good greeting is straightforward. Although there is, fortunately, no pat "have a good day" type of phrase for welcoming individuals, all good greetings do tend to share certain elements. The good greeting

quickly acknowledges the patron's presence, even if the staff member cannot immediately attend to the patron's needs;

focuses attention on the individual patron;

includes some sign of encouragement (such as a nod or smile) and avoids any evidence of annoyance or exhaustion;

is offered by a person who looks competent/professional— i.e., is well-groomed, seems engaged in some work activity, and is not snacking in a service area.

In short, the good greeting assures the patron that she has reached someone who will help her. Simply heightening staff sensitivity to the need for a positive greeting and to the elements of such a greeting is usually enough to inspire gracious greetings.

Identifying the Patron's Need

The next stage in basic service is identifying the patron's need. Whether a staff member is working at the reference desk or in bindery preparation, each person should be required to review the elements of careful listening. The following techniques can help reassure any help-seeking individual. Good listening skills include

paying attention to the words, expressions, and body language of the speaker;

using body language to express your continued concentration on the speaker by nodding or leaning forward;

uttering some simple phrase such as "I see," or "Go on";

permitting the speaker to hold the floor;

---

1. Karl Albrecht and Ron Zemke, *Service America! Doing Business in the New Economy* (Homewood, Ill: Dow Jones-Irwin, 1985), 31.

asking brief questions and using rephrasing to test your understanding of the patron's actual desire.

Responding to the Need

After the staff member has identified what a patron really wants, it is time to offer help. Although some organizations prescribe the type of help they want their library staff to deliver (i.e., instruction for students, exhaustive research for legislators, or minimal help for unaffiliated users), a flexible service style is more useful. To maximize staff ability to meet any individual's need, staff members should be encouraged to offer a range of options. For instance:

> "You can use this volume to quickly identify a few popular magazine articles on sexual harassment, or I can show you how to use a CD product to find more scholarly material."

> "I can have that book rush cataloged for you in three days, or I can arrange for you to use it here in the library right now."

> "I can give you change when our cash register is open, or you can use the change machine in the basement."

> "You can pay the fine with cash or a check, ask for more time to search for the missing item, or speak to the supervisor about this matter."

Involving the patron in satisfying her need or resolving a problem makes it more likely that she will like the solution. Although staff may benefit from reading about models of ideal service and role-playing experiences, they should realize that quality service is not a polished performance of practiced phrases; it is finding a feasible solution that pleases your patron. No matter how many examples of desirable service you crowd into your training manual, it is impossible to fully describe for staff what good service will look like in all possible situations. One description offered by Joel Carter at a training program on exceptional customer service was that good service earns a "thank you." Carter urges trainers to advise their staff to "always try to win a thank you." Carter stressed that people say "thank you" when they feel that they have been treated pleasantly and fairly and have been offered something of value.[2]

Following Up

The patron's expression of gratitude does not always mark the end of a successful encounter. A few patrons will never offer a hint of appreciation for even the most heroic service. Far more common, however, are undemanding patrons who quickly thank staff for any kind of assistance.

To make certain that your service is effective as well as cordial, encourage your staff to build follow-up mechanisms into their work routines. Although these mechanisms can include formal surveys and patron interviews, the casual approach may be the most effective. A parting line such as "If this source doesn't supply all of the information you need, please let me know" or "Please stop back if you have any more questions" can convince even timid patrons to pursue their questions.

Planning Aid

Create a story representing a troublesome scenario that your staff member is likely to face at some point. For instance, a patron asks to check out your latest *Statistical Abstract of the United States*, a volume too popular to circulate. Then ask your trainee to develop five responses that will keep that volume in the library but will earn a sincere patron vote of thanks.

---

2. Joel Carter, *Exceptional Customer Service* (Workshop offered by Dun & Bradstreet, South Bend, Ind., Dec. 1991).

CHAPTER SIX

Expanding the Definition of Patrons

A T TIMES STAFF ACT as if the only patrons who count are the bland Brand X patrons. The good patron is a hard-working, quiet yet articulate soul, who walks into the library, describes an interesting, serious, and reasonable need, and who appreciates what the library has to offer. In training staff to deal with the public, point out that the public is not homogenized. Library clienteles vary, but user populations include many or all of the following: persons of different ages; power patrons who help fund or run your library; latchkey children deposited by busy parents; mail, phone, e-mail, and fax patrons; disabled or specially challenged individuals; internationals for whom English is a second language; the indigent and the homeless; poor readers and the illiterate; slow thinkers; and stump-the-librarian gamesters. Tailor the training program so that your staff is prepared for the many faces of your patrons, informed about their special needs, and trained on how to respond to these needs.

For each category of patron that your staff is likely to meet, prepare a training module based on the following model for phone patrons.

Completed Sample Training Module:
Telephone Patrons

1. **Describe a patron type that your staff members are likely to encounter.**

   Many service staff view phone patrons as pests rather than as clients to be helped. These faceless voices sometimes come across as lazy, demanding, or annoying, and staff may give them second-class treatment.

2. **Help the employee see this individual as part of the primary clientele.**

   Your training program should combat stereotypes and remind your staff that these voices belong to patrons every bit as important as walk-in clients they may consider their first responsibility. Give the staff member a copy of the library's guidelines for service to this group (if such a policy has been written), or describe the library's service commitment and resources for special service.

   A phone patron should receive the same high level of courtesy and service as on-site patrons. Although desk pressures may force an employee to juggle patrons, to place a caller on hold, or to return a call, the phone patron should always feel as if the employee cares about her need and will help her. The guidelines listed below suggest responses for common scenarios.

   Phone rings at service desk.

   Recommended response: Answer phone by the third ring. Turn your attention to the caller as if you were greeting a walk-in patron and identify yourself and your unit. Communicate a cheerful, businesslike attitude through tone of voice and receptive attitude.

   Phone rings while you are helping an on-site patron.

   Recommended response: The best choice is for the manager to avoid this conflict by having all phone calls transferred to a nonservice desk site either immediately or after the third ring. Another solution is to take advantage of the hold features of your institution's phone-mail system or to use an answering machine.

It is important to stop the phone's ringing. Excuse yourself from the patron and answer the phone. Tell the phone patron that you are helping another patron at this moment and ask her to hold or offer to transfer her to a nondesk service number. If you do put a patron on hold, get back to her promptly. If you anticipate not being able to return to the caller quickly, offer to take her name and number and phone her later.

Phone patron wants you to look up ready-reference information.

Recommended response: It is important for new staff to have some guidelines that indicate how much time to give a phone patron, i.e., five catalog-information questions or twenty minutes of research. The best approach, however, is to model phone service on desk service and allow it to fluctuate according to demands. Although it may be necessary to ask a patron to wait for a follow-up call or to come into the library for certain types of assistance, these requests should be based on a genuine need rather than on a set policy.

You don't know the answer to the phone patron's question.

Recommended response: If you know who has the answer, offer the patron the individual's phone number, and transfer her to that person or unit. If you do not know where to get the answer, tell the patron that you want to do some research before making a referral so that she is spared a series of blind referrals.

Patron's question requires follow-up.

Recommended response: Describe the level of follow-up service that can be provided, the anticipated time frame for a response, and any costs that might be involved. Be certain to get an accurate name and phone number for the patron and give her your name and number.

Phone requests should be followed up in twenty-four hours, even if the follow-up only involves calling the patron to report that you have found nothing. A procedure should be in place to ensure prompt follow-up phone calls. It should include provisions for times when it is not possible to reach patrons with a return call. One solution would be to post a note on the desk communications sheet stating whatever information you were able or not able to locate and making sure that it is someone's duty to follow through on additional call-back attempts.

3. **Ask the employee to read a specific article or to watch a selected video on the experiences or service needs of the patron group being studied.**

    Following are some sample training aids for dealing with telephone customers.

    The *Telephone Doctor Video Training Series* offers excellent tapes on telephone skills and customer service. Titles such as "Five Forbidden Phrases," "From Curt to Courteous," and "How to Treat Every Caller as a Welcome Guest" are available for preview, rental, or purchase from The Telephone Doctor, 12119 St. Charles Road, St. Louis, MO 63044.

    Yates, Rochelle. *A Librarian's Guide to Telephone Reference Service.* Hamden, Conn.: Library Professional Publications, 1986.

4. **Develop a case study demonstrating some of the special problems faced by this category of the patron group under consideration, and ask the employee to identify some possible responses.**

    Training several staff members at once provides an opportunity for role playing, which helps staff recognize patronizing or unresponsive answers. Following is a sample case study scenario.

    You are working alone at a very busy information desk at Green County Public Library. The mayor's secretary calls and says that the mayor needs the names and addresses of the publishers of about twenty periodicals and that she needs it now. Although the source of this information is at your service desk, the information will require multiple look-ups. Furthermore, you see three restless patrons circling your desk area. Identify three ways to handle this call that could satisfy the mayor and tend to your on-site patrons.

Planning Aid

Ask one or more experienced staff members from technical services to prepare a training module focusing on one specific staff or patron group that frequently asks for special service. For example, this staff/patron group may be your branch librarians or staff from another technical service area. Individuals drafting the training module should involve other technical service staff in discussing approaches to service and should coach new staff in meeting agreed-upon standards.

CHAPTER SEVEN

Teaching Staff to Sell Library Services

L IBRARIANS KNOW that many patrons don't recognize what the library has to offer. Banners, posters, neon signs, and hypertext training aids may attract the attention of a few individuals, but most patrons come to the library with a specific need in mind and tend to follow set patterns in their work. Only when your frontline staff say, "Our document delivery service can rush that article to your office" are patrons likely to try out a new service. The manager's training job is to prepare staff to promote library services.

Advertise Within

Staff can't sell what they don't know. Make certain that all of your staff know what services your library offers. If you deliver materials to the homebound or offer selective dissemination of information, showcase these services for your staff. Use workshops, tours, demonstrations, and staff newsletters to educate staff in the scope of services offered by your library.

If your library is large or if it offers a particularly large number of specialized services, create a directory highlighting these services. Armed with such a tool, all staff will be prepared at any point to tell the searching patron where to go for assistance or whom to ask.

Sell Your Staff on New Services

Staff won't promote a service that intimidates them. Before you ask staff to deliver a new service, build in time for testing and training. This is particularly important in this age of technological wonders and miracles, when at times the promised miracle doesn't occur and no one knows why. Preparing your staff can save them from embarrassment, increase their support for the new system, and safeguard your patrons as well. For the sake of staff and patrons alike, follow the advice offered by Laura A. Liswood in *Serving Them Right*, "Never let your customers be Guinea Pigs!"[1] Don't ask your staff to sell untested services.

Protect Staff from Service Overload

From the perspective of the staff member, the promotion of new products and services often is the beginning of a downward spiral, shown in figure 2.

Staff need to know that they are safe from this scenario. The manager must provide some visible, reliable mechanisms of support that demonstrate that successful service promotion is not self-destructive.

Show staff that the department is ready to respond to growing demands. If good service generates higher work loads, provide relief. Use a "floater" position to assist areas facing new work loads. Create a special-work-attack team composed of flexible staff who are ready and eager to relieve an overstressed unit. Prioritize work in progress. Low-priority work can be deferred or eliminated to make more time for first-priority projects. Establish a discretionary fund to hire on-call help as needed. All of these measures can assure staff that it is safe to encourage patron demands.

---

1. Laura A. Liswood, *Serving Them Right: Innovative and Powerful Customer Retention Strategies* (New York: Harper and Row, 1990), 55.

Figure 2. Super-Service Backlash

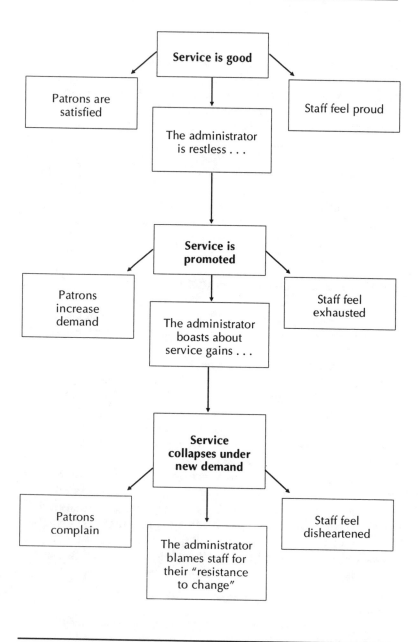

Make it easy for your staff to warn you at the first sign that service demands are outstripping available resources. Surprisingly, some staff hesitate to report backlogs for fear of being perceived as complainers. Intervene promptly by finding new funding, shifting resources, altering priorities, or upgrading equipment. Give your staff the support they need to keep your library's service promises. If adequate funding is simply not available, alert your users. Although you should always guard against embarrassing your administrators, you should tell patrons when they need to modify their expectations. A notice, such as "Due to increases in the postal rate, we now charge for interlibrary loans," can ease pressures on your staff and forewarn your patrons.

Charge $$$ for Special Services

It may be necessary to charge fees, recover costs, or limit use of certain services. Although charges may seem like a disservice, they may be the only viable way of supporting certain costly activities and protecting the quality of others. Even modest fees can encourage patrons to weigh carefully requests for interlibrary loans, document delivery, or online searching. To ease the impact on low-income patrons, the library might introduce charges on a scale that recognizes the differing research demands of different student levels and academic departments. Patrons needing extra services, such as express mail or translation, are likely to prefer paying a fee to losing the service.

Planning Aid

Prepare a list of special services that patrons might request, and ask the trainees to identify the providers of these services within your library. You may wish to expand this list to include resources and services in your organization, on your campus, or in your county.

CHAPTER EIGHT

Empowering Staff

STAFF AT EVERY LEVEL of the organization should understand that library policies were created to help patrons, not to interfere with service. Policies should keep the library functioning smoothly, meeting most patrons' needs without seriously harming any one patron.

At times, however, patrons will have special needs that can be met by exercising a little judgment and flexibility. All staff should know that policies can be bent by someone at some level at some time. Individual libraries will set their own levels of empowerment, but all staff should remember the warning from the National Institute of Business Management training workbook, "Never tell the patron . . . there's nothing I can do. That's our policy."[1]

Empowering the staff takes training, planning, and experience. In most cases a manager must establish levels of empowerment, clarify these levels, coach staff in problem solving, and be prepared to accept errors as well as alternative solutions to problems.

---

1. National Institute of Business Management, *Service and Satisfaction: A Frontline Employee's Workbook* (New York: NIBM, 1989), 29.

New staff need more guidelines than old employees. Each individual and situation combine to require a slightly different use of empowerment. To organize your training, however, it might be useful to identify three basic levels of empowerment and to aim your training at one of these levels.

Define Levels of Empowerment

The minimum level of empowerment might be reserved for staff who work very limited schedules, such as volunteer workers or student staff. Because these individuals may not have a comprehensive understanding of ongoing demands on the library or may lack, through their part-time status, an overview of departmental operations, they may not be able to judge special patron requests. Therefore, these staff may be asked not to bend policies. They should, however, be reminded not to say "no." When faced with a patron with a special need, they should refer to the individual trained to interpret the policy.

The moderate level of empowerment should guide most nonsupervisory staff. This level permits staff members to bend policy within certain guidelines, for instance, to forgive fines up to $10 or to permit a reference book to circulate for three days. Other allowances might include accepting work from an internal patron via phone rather than insisting on the use of a specific form or phoning in an order rather than mailing it to speed the acquisitions process. Your frontline people should protect your patrons against unnecessary bureaucracy and departmental politics and be guided by the clear primary objective: to satisfy the customer.[2]

Staff at the managerial level are expected to improvise to meet the needs of the patron. The manager is responsible for understanding the needs of the patron and for determining if there is any reasonable way in which the library can satisfy this patron. Improvisation may mean ordering materials and having them sent by Federal Express, sending someone to a local bookstore to get needed materials, adding special hours, or reorganizing parts of

---

2. Laura A. Liswood, *Serving Them Right: Innovative and Powerful Customer Retention Strategies* (New York: Harper and Row, 1990), 3.

the collection to make them more user friendly. Although she cannot meet every patron need, the manager must take each need seriously and search for an acceptable solution.

Before you empower staff, you must prepare them to deal with problem solving. Successful empowerment programs include four elements: familiarity with policies, skill training, practice, and follow-up.

Increase Familiarity with Policies

To prepare your staff to interpret policies, start by providing them with a clear statement of pertinent policies in written form and readily available for consultation. Critical policies (such as the statement on the confidentiality of patron records) should include a concluding statement identifying the "official policy interpreter," the arbiter of special situations for the department or the library. When training staff to apply policies, you should also prepare staff for likely challenges and exceptions. Discussing exceptions at staff meetings is helpful. A staff member who knows why a policy was written and how it has been interpreted is well-prepared to make a reasonable judgment.

Offer Listening and Problem-Solving Skills Training

Knowing your library's policies and potential exceptions can help staff assist patrons. Interpreting policies, however, takes a special set of skills. To understand what the patron really wants, staff need exceptional listening skills. The staff member should be taught to listen for the patron's description of her need, the urgency of the request, and the patron's comfort in using library resources. Does she want a short, popular article or an in-depth research study?

Although the staff member need not agree with the patron's own evaluation of her need, the staff member should be trained to express some sensitivity toward the patron's feelings. If a circulation patron says that her library books were stolen from her unlocked car, offer her some sympathy rather than a lecture on responsibility. It is useful for staff to remember that understanding someone and recognizing her feelings does not necessarily mean agreeing with her.

Staff will also need some training on problem solving. Careful preparation can help staff identify ways to satisfy the patron without overcommitting the library or disrupting service to other users. No one can write scenarios for all of the problems that patrons will present. The best a trainer can do is offer an employee some tips on problem resolution. Some useful suggestions include:

- Don't explain why you can't do what the customer wants. Instead, describe what you can do.

- When faced with what seems like an unsolvable problem, try describing it in some alternative ways. Sometimes the vocabulary rather than the concept is the actual block.

- Focus on the customer's point of view. Take the customer's side, not the company's, for a few moments.

- Search for a solution that will earn a genuine expression of thanks from the patron.[3]

- Ask the patron to suggest some acceptable compromise.

- Offer the patron some options and permit the patron to select the most acceptable of these options.

Provide Skills Practice

Preparing staff to negotiate problems requires practice as well as theory. Offer new staff a chance to discuss several case studies, such as those shown in figure 3, before they are asked to cope with real-life situations. This will save your staff from struggling in front of patrons and will permit your patrons to "get what they came in for without having to stumble through a trial-and-error exercise with a poorly prepared trainee."[4]

---

3. Joel Carter, *Exceptional Customer Service* (Workshop offered by Dun & Bradstreet, South Bend, Ind., Dec. 1991).
4. Liswood, *Serving Them Right*, 51.

Figure 3. Case Studies

Directions: Some of these case studies are written from a staff member's point of view and others are written from the patron's perspective. Pick any three cases and consider them from your group perspective as staff or as patrons and describe how you would like to see the case handled.

> *Staff:* How would you approach these situations? What questions would you ask, if any? What would you do, if anything?

> *Patrons:* How would you want the librarian to handle these situations? What could be said or done that would be acceptable to you and considerate of other users?

Case 1

Pat Patron has been using the library's only copy of PAIS (a compact disc reference index) for ten minutes. Three students have approached the desk asking to use PAIS. You see the students milling around the reference area while Pat Patron pores over PAIS. What do you do? (To provoke some interesting discussions, offer staff different descriptions for Pat Patron such as a senior member of the faculty, a local business person, or a young person from the local homeless shelter.)

Case 2

You are working on claiming undelivered supplies. The director of libraries suddenly appears at your desk with a copy of the development plan report and says, "I need to have twelve copies of this in time for my 9:30 administrators' meeting." You look at the forty-page report and realize that you will have to work at top speed to meet the director's need. You leave the outer office unattended and begin the photocopying. You have only finished the first eight pages when a graduate student pokes her head in the workroom and asks, "Anyone home?"

The student explains that she has three telefax messages from Professor Scarlet that must be sent immediately. Professor Scarlet's colleague is standing by in New York waiting for these documents. The libraries' fax policy promises that fax requests will be sent out within two hours. It is now 8:45. You estimate that it will take you 40 to 45 minutes to finish the director's photocopying and that it would take fifteen minutes to fax these multipage documents. What would you do?

Case 3

A junior faculty member from the life sciences department comes into the Chemistry/Physics Library at nine o'clock on a Friday morning. She has her two-year-old daughter with her. She quickly moves around the library gathering up the latest issues of the most popular journals in her area of research. While she is pulling these titles off the shelves, she is also busy chasing and hushing her energetic, noisy daughter. Finally, the faculty member brings an armful of journals to your desk and says, "I want to take these home."

While watching her daughter spill her sack of treats, you tell the faculty member that current journals do not circulate. The faculty member says that she doesn't care what your policy is, she needs these journals, her child needs to go home, and she must meet the deadline for submitting this article for publication. As you look at the out-of-order sign on your only copying machine, the little girl begins to cry, the phone begins to ring, and you notice two graduate students glaring at the commotion. You reflect on the stack of very popular journals, the crying child, the glaring graduate students, and the angry faculty member. What do you do?

Case 4

You are trying to help the world's most unlucky patron. She has brought you a list of fourteen journal articles about psychology and caffeinated soft drinks. Three journals are at the bindery, two are lost, four articles are in journals which the library doesn't own, and two articles have been ripped out of their volumes. You have (with a prayer) sent the patron to the stacks to retrieve two articles in bound journals. Now you are trying to track down the last article so you can have something to offer the patron when and if she returns. This volume has been sent to the cataloging department awaiting relabeling. You call the labeler's number only to learn she is out ill today. A staff member from another unit in cataloging has answered the phone. What do you say?

Case 5

You are a reference librarian who is trying to help patrons with the department's newest online product. This afternoon, technology seems to be taunting you as the images fade, printers jam, and keyword searches retrieve mysterious results. The phone rings and a woman with a very high-pitched voice begins telling you her problems. She has to get her department head some biographical information on four potential speakers so the department head can discuss them at a meeting in one hour. Since she is alone in the office, she simply cannot get in to the library. She called the business librarian, but he won't be back at the library until the evening shift. The caller seems extremely agitated. She confides that she has made a few mistakes this morning and really must deliver on this request from the department head.

Case 6

Staff member Kelly has sent you a supplies order form and has failed to complete the bottom half of the form as required. While the information in the bottom half is useful for planning, it is not critical for you to have it to order the proper supplies. Kelly rarely orders supplies anyway. What should you do?

Case 7

You do all of the cataloging and catalog maintenance work for a midsized corporate library. Two months ago, the reference group at your library asked you to alter records for 400 annual reports as they were shifted into an annex. After seven weeks of review, they have decided that the annex was not a secure area and have asked you to return the reports to the original location. If they had made this new request in a polite, somewhat apologetic, and clear manner, you might have been sympathetic while explaining that you now are pressed by three other high-priority projects. Unfortunately, the request was made in the worst possible manner. In a public meeting that included your boss and library patrons, one of these reference librarians turned to you and said, "If cataloging cares about service, you have to get those records changed by next week or our collections will be stripped of the most valuable titles." What is your reaction?

Follow-Up on Training

Empowering staff is a never-ending process. Following up on training is essential. In individual conferences and in staff meetings, continue to offer encouragement and support. The departmental staff as a group should discuss recent situations and alternative ways of addressing them. There are no perfect solutions. The approach that is successful for one patron and one staff member may not work for another pair. Regular discussion of situations and solutions plays an important role in educating staff about available service options. Examining a variety of perspectives on a single situation can encourage staff to try alternatives rather than to cling to one safe response.

Planning Aid

Define minimum, moderate, and manager levels of empowerment for your library.

CHAPTER NINE

Encouraging Good Service on Bad Days

GOOD TRAINING plus good intentions does not always equal good service. Bad days come, staff members have headaches and black moods, children choose the library as their rainy-day haven, the CD-ROM player spits out discs instead of playing them, and crabby patrons come in spoiling for a fight. Because these days are inevitable, the manager should help new staff prepare for them. Preparation involves training and planning.

Dealing with Grumpy, Sick Staff

Everyone can have a bad day. Colds, sore feet, broken hearts, visiting in-laws, traffic jams, and major crises can unsettle even the most sanguine of spirits. Train your staff to recognize and adjust to bad days.

In *The Service Edge*, Ron Zemke and Dick Schaaf describe some approaches used at Disneyland to prepare staff for dealing with service pressure. Library managers can take a tip from the trainers at the Magic Kingdom. Staff there are told that they are actors and that the park is their stage. Whether they are hired to sweep the grounds or sell balloons, they are expected to be "on" when they step from their staff facilities into the park. For them, being "on" means smiling; being well-groomed; smiling; not eating, drinking, or smoking; smiling; offering informed assistance; and smiling.[1]

It may not be realistic to expect such a bubbly appearance from your staff, but you can remind your staff that they should adopt a public demeanor when they are "on." You should also teach your supervisors to develop strategies to relieve pressure and to alert their staff to these releases. All staff should know that the manager understands there are hours or days when a staff member needs special consideration. Sheltering a stressed staff member from pressures for a short time can ease frustration and avoid damaging and time-consuming conflicts.

It is important, however, to keep in mind that no matter how out-of-sorts a person may feel, taking it out on patrons is *never* acceptable. No matter how rude a patron may be, it is *never* permissible to be rude in return.

Handling Disruptive Patrons

Libraries are made to house books and provide access to information. Unfortunately some patrons see the library as a place in which they can listen to music, snack on pizza and beer, and engage in a range of activities better suited for anywhere else.

Although librarians want to make the library inviting, library managers do have a responsibility to prepare their staff to protect library users and collections. Managers must offer their public services staff guidelines and training for dealing with disruptive patrons. It is also important to identify the appropriate office or individuals to call for security assistance. Encourage your staff to approach disruptive patrons in a polite and positive manner. Ask your staff to identify tactful phrases that might be used to replace dictums, such as "This is a library; please maintain silence" or "You will have to get rid of that coffee now." Each employee can find a phrase that feels natural to him, but all employees should understand that phrasing can make or break a request. Most

---

1. Ron Zemke with Dick Schaaf, *The Service Edge: 101 Companies That Profit from Customer Care* (New York: New American Library, 1989), 532.

patrons will comply with a courteous and reasonable request such as the following:

> "Excuse me, Miss." (The tone of this initial contact should generally be gentle, indicating that you truly regret interrupting someone's work to tell them about a policy that they surely did not know.)
>
> "This area of the library is for quiet study" (or reference collections, fragile magazines, patrons who are reading, nonsmokers, etc.).
>
> "If you wish to listen to your radio, you may use the lounge or patio, or you may check out some materials to take to a place where you would feel more comfortable."

A few patrons, however, will refuse to respond or will resume their activities as soon as the employee walks away. Assertiveness training techniques can help the staff member at this point. In their book, *Responsible Assertive Behavior*, Arthur J. Lange and Patricia Jakubowski advise individuals to strengthen their forcefulness by using nonverbal techniques such as looking at the other person; speaking in a fluent, clear, and expressive manner that stresses key words; and using a firm tone.[2] Standing near the patron and assuming a solid-looking, flat-footed manner can help demonstrate a staff member's seriousness.

Using these nonverbal techniques and reasserting the request may well win patron cooperation. You must, however, prepare your staff for those cases in which the patron refuses to budge. At this point the staff member should offer a final warning that he is now going to contact the security office or individual for your library. (This may be the library director, campus security, the local police, or some other designated body.) The staff member should warn the patron, "I'm being left with no alternative but to call security. I'd rather not do that, but I am obligated to protect our collections." After making this statement, the staff member should call the designated security person or office if the patron still refuses to cooperate.

---

2. Arthur J. Lange and Patricia Jakubowski, *Responsible Assertive Behavior: Cognitive/Behavioral Procedures for Trainers* (Champaign, Ill.: Research Press, 1976), 10–12.

Although staff should be trained to deal with patrons who break library rules or are disruptive, library staff should not be asked to serve as "bouncers." Managers should caution their employees not to approach patrons who seem dangerous or out of control. These cases should be turned over immediately to security staff.

Saying "No" to the Patron

Although a manager may want her staff to be service-oriented and to strive to meet patron needs, staff will inevitably have to tell some patrons "no." Library resources are finite and can be depleted rapidly by overwhelming or unreasonable patron demands. Train your staff to soften the "no" when possible by

offering some partial accommodation, i.e., "I can have one of the titles you need rush cataloged for you today, but I cannot rush catalog all of your orders."

demonstrating their genuine regret that no acceptable solution has been found. (If a staff member begins to feel delight at saying "no," it may well be time to take him away from the service counter. Library staff are not hired to punish patrons, but to serve them.)

providing some explanation. The service worker who has searched for a way of saying "yes" and who truly wants to help the patron, should have a clear idea of why the answer is "no." Although the patron will not always agree with the explanation, the patron does deserve the respect shown by a considered response, such as, "A class of forty has been assigned to read that book so I cannot allow any individual to have it for the weekend."

After offering an alternative, demonstrating concern, and providing an explanation for a refusal, the staff member has fulfilled his responsibility. If the patron continues to argue, the staff member should use assertive techniques to politely but firmly restate the "no." It is not necessary or fruitful to jump into a prolonged defense; it is appropriate to refer the dissatisfied patron to the administration.

Coping with Angry Patrons

Patrons from the two previous categories, disruptive patrons and those to whom you must say "no," may turn into angry patrons. All staff should be prepared to cope with these irate persons. The manager must teach her staff to distance themselves from patron anger. According to the National Institute of Business Management, one of the first rules in coping with irate patrons is *"Don't be defensive."*[3] The staff member must remember that the patron is not really angry with him but is upset by a policy or series of circumstances. A patron's anger is rarely personally focused but more often echoes frustration with the system.

To help staff view angry patrons more objectively, offer your staff some defusing techniques. Videos, readings, and workshops can give them the skills needed to calm an irate patron, identify the problem, and secure relief.

Calming the Patron

Calming the patron is the most demanding of the defusing steps. It requires self-control, patience, and strong interpersonal skills. Although you cannot teach personality attributes, you can offer your staff concrete suggestions on diminishing patron fury.

The service worker's first goal is to move the encounter from an attack to a discussion. The best approach is to get the patron into an office or at least into a sitting area in a less-public location. Most patrons will respond to a phrase such as, "Let's step into my office for a few moments so we can solve this problem." Ideally, an office or area can be provided for this eventuality.

Once the patron is in a quiet area, the staff member should offer that patron his full attention. The job at this point is to permit the patron to express her feelings. A very irate patron generally is not ready to begin negotiation. First, she must be heard. Encourage staff to try to understand the experience from the patron's perspective. Although you do not want a staff member to join the patron in attacking another staff member or unit of the library, it is important to listen in a nondefensive mode. Instead of dwelling on the angry tone, the staff member should strive to

---

3. National Institute of Business Management, *Service and Satisfaction: A Frontline Employee's Workbook* (New York: NIBM, 1989), 21.

understand what has upset the patron and why. As he listens, the staff member should imagine himself in the patron's position and search for areas of agreement.

Identifying the Problem

After the patron has voiced some of her anger and frustration, staff should begin to move the discussion to a less-emotional level. Some techniques that can help your staff gain the individual's attention and cooperation are addressing the individual by name, expressing some appreciation for the individual's feelings, and indicating some area of agreement.

Practice, regular reminders, and group discussion can help staff perfect their skills in dealing with upset patrons. To prepare the new employee, teach him one technique that can be used to diffuse many situations. Ask staff to offer upset individuals some sign of agreement. A simple "You're right" soothes more effectively than fifty clever explanations. Although it is difficult to agree with a hostile patron, the goal is to win cooperation, not triumph in a competition.

Once the patron begins to trust a staff member as a listener, that employee has a chance to explore the problem. He will need to ask questions to understand the situation, but he should guard against slipping into the role of the grand inquisitor. A series of questions even in the best circumstance can raise another's defensiveness. Staff should be advised to work with patrons to develop a mutual definition of the precise problem. Agreeing on the nature of the problem prepares both parties to agree on a solution.

Providing Relief

Ask your staff to focus their attention on resolving the patron's problem in a mutually satisfactory manner. You must prepare your staff to deal with tough situations before the situations develop. Offer staff insightful articles and books. Encourage group discussions highlighting examples of staff calming or helping patrons. Encourage staff to take credit for resolving conflicts, but guard against war stories about staff triumphing over patrons. Although you cannot prepare staff for every situation, offer the staff some written descriptions of likely situations and reasonable responses. Some sample scenarios follow.

When an obvious library mistake has upset a patron, advise your staff to admit the error. Although you should protect the staff and library from abusive accusations, there is no reason to cling to an aura of perfection. Capable and well-meaning staff do make mistakes. Vendors, publishers, and binders, not to mention copiers, computers, and CD players, also disrupt service. If the library is at fault, the staff member needs to acknowledge the error, correct the error, and offer an apology. Although this response will satisfy most patrons, the library should consider going one step farther. For instance, the staff member might want to offer the patron some type of compensation for the trouble. A copy card good for ten free copies or even the phone number of the staff member with the statement, "Call me personally if you ever need special assistance in our library," can turn an angry patron into a library booster.

A tougher situation is when the patron is at fault. Some patrons simply don't want to hear that they have overdue materials, owe fines, or have to leave at closing time. In working with these patrons, train staff to avoid voicing any judgments and to focus on the concrete problem. Offering information and asking patrons for suggestions can help resolve the concern in a diplomatic manner.

In the worst scenarios, the patron will not let go of her state of rage. Managers should make certain that their unit heads and staff know what to do with abusive clientele. Staff should have some easy-to-remember guidelines, such as:

- Call the patron by name (if known) to get her attention.
- Direct the patron's attention away from venting her emotions. Encourage her to focus on factual details related to the problem. ("Please spell the author's name so I can check on your order.")
- Ask the patron firmly, but politely, to move from name calling, etc., to working on the problem.
- Offer to contact your supervisor so that the two of them can meet.

Although the manager should prepare staff to work with upset individuals, it is equally important that she train staff when and how to refer patrons to her, another supervisor, or security personnel. Whether the patron demands to talk to the "boss" or the staff member chooses to refer the individual, the staff member should ease the transition. One important technique that will facilitate this process is to call the supervisor before sending the patron to her office. This simple step can save an already furious patron from arriving at an empty office and can prepare the supervisor to deal with the patron. You may want to train your staff to make two calls: one made in the presence of the irate patron alerting the supervisor that the patron would like to talk to her and the other to privately explain the details of the situation. Remember that the employee is never required to endure abusive or threatening behavior. The employee's safety is always of first concern.

Fortunately few patrons remain irate for long. Individuals engaged in a dialogue seek a common level of tone. If the listener can resist matching the intense level of the complainer, the complainer will very quickly drop to the tone of the listener. This tip can be very reassuring to the staff member facing his first furious patron.

Planning Aid

Prepare your own guidelines for dealing with abusive patrons. At what point and to whom do you want your staff to refer these patrons? At what point should security be called? If you have not done so recently, schedule a meeting with the head of the security department or, in the case of a public library, the local police. Ask the security personnel for their recommendations for dealing with specific problematic situations.

CHAPTER TEN

Maintaining a Long-Term Service Commitment

PROVIDING QUALITY SERVICE must be an ongoing commitment. To make this commitment work, it must extend beyond the training period, involve staff at all levels, and be tied to rewards and recognition. Each level of management should make certain that supervisors are trained to continue the commitment.

Keep the Focus on Service

As a manager or as a trainer of managers, you can strengthen the impact of service training by removing it from the isolated world of theory and linking service to the daily tasks and situations that are part of your library. *Keeping Customers for Life* by Joan Koob Cannie with Donald Caplin offers numerous suggestions for keeping service in the minds of staff throughout their careers. Cannie writes:

- "Make service quality and customer satisfaction a key part of the agenda at meetings. Spend at least as much time discussing them as you do costs, production, planning, schedules, and innovation.

- "Communicate your commitment in every publication.
- "All of your systems, policies, and decisions send messages to customers. Are they friendly? Or do they send 'We don't trust you' or 'We're adversaries' or 'You're a pest' messages?"[1]

Additional ways to highlight service include holding service-givers training sessions and discussion groups that focus on issues such as helping the disabled patron or dealing with requests for information in nontraditional formats; creating service-impact statements to accompany budget requests, system changes, and budget cuts; and describing budget priorities and administrative decisions in terms of their impact on service.

It is particularly important that staff at the line level hear the explanations for budget decisions. They have not been privy to the agonizing discussion about which services have to be sacrificed or reduced to salvage some vital operations. Cryptic announcements stating that hours must be cut or that the writing of call numbers on order slips must be eliminated to save time can be easily misinterpreted. Left to the staff's imagination, explanations may materialize that label other staff as lazy or managers as misguided. It is not important that all staff support your choices, but it is important for them to see you basing your choices on your service commitments.

Involve Staff at All Levels

At every level of your organization, staff should hear about service and see evidence of its importance. From the interview forward, make certain that each staff member feels involved in trying to improve service. Training should emphasize the fact that the people on the front line and those creating records, files, and collections to support the front line have invaluable insights that can make the organization excel.

Service excellence depends on the library's staff. Staff, not cloistered administrators, are in the best position to hear library

---

1. Joan Koob Cannie with Donald Caplin, *Keeping Customers for Life* (New York: American Management Association, 1991), 140.

patrons muttering about specific library policies and procedures. During the training period, prepare staff to champion patron needs. Urge them to listen to patrons and to identify and report problems with policies, procedures, or collections and to document patron complaints and suggestions. Staff should know that reporting in-house problems, such as backlogs and delays, will win them praise and assistance, not criticism.

In a sense, staff should feel that their managers are working for them. During the training process and thereafter, staff should be encouraged to tell management what they need to get their work done and how management can make this an easier process. The focus in a service organization is not on pleasing the management, but on pleasing the patron.

Most important of all, managers should make certain that their staff see managers practicing what they preach. In dealing with the staff, managers must demonstrate the caring, respect, flexibility, and strong interpersonal skills that they require from the staff. Furthermore, the manager should be seen actually helping real patrons. This does not mean that every library director must spend x hours working at a service point, but it does mean that the director should help patrons in front of staff. Whenever the opportunity arises, the director or manager should be ready to show service in action. Whether one is answering a phone at an unstaffed desk, referring a patron to the appropriate department, assuming responsibility for an irate patron, or responding to a misdirected call, the staff will be watching the manager as model. Make the message clear that no one is *above* giving service. Example is a powerful training tool. Managers can also assist staff by taking policy-related incidents into consideration and revising policies or procedures that cause more problems than they solve.

Recognize Service Achievements

You need not embrace every interpretation of Pavlov to recognize that rewards do reinforce training. Ron Zemke and Dick Schaaf's outstanding work, *The Service Edge*, lists five operating principles of service. The fifth principle, "recognize and reward accomplishments," provides critical support for the other four goals. "Recognizing and praising employees for a job well done . . . is a confirmation of accomplishment and a reinforcement of commitment."[2] Zemke points out that successful service companies reward staff for meeting service standards and make heroes out of staff who exceed these standards. In one way or the other, all of the service literature reminds managers to recognize staff accomplishments. Successful service organizations build in multiple methods of rewards and always welcome new ones.

Recognition and reward can be accomplished in private and public ways. Although few managers would want to use a phrase such as "atta boy" to encourage their employees, the concept of offering a staff member a short, encouraging phrase, such as "Quick thinking, Phil," remains highly effective. Train your supervisors to listen to their staff and to reinforce service-oriented actions quickly. Supervisors should encourage staff to take pride in their ability to deal with demanding patrons and to develop creative solutions for a series of problems.

Accomplishments should be publicized. During staff meetings, praise individuals or units for some particular achievement. Did interlibrary loan just improve its fill rate by 5 percent? Did the staff member in life sciences use a flashlight in a windowless library to help desperate patrons get materials during a power failure? Did the acquisitions librarian acquire a needed volume in twenty-four hours? Don't just thank the individuals, tell the division or the entire library about their achievements. Use printed newsletters and bulletin boards to highlight service accomplishments. List goals, such as how many days a department can go without a serial check-in error or how many days it will take to bar code a branch collection, and chart the success on a public scoreboard. Print statistics that show growing service numbers and shrinking backlogs. Publish patron comments praising unit efforts.

Staff performance evaluations are an important way of recognizing individual staff members' accomplishments. Make certain that every staff performance evaluation includes some sincere and honest comments on service. Use whatever mechanisms are available to you to reward service. Ideally, salary increments and promotions should be tied to service successes. If your company, institution, or library rules do not provide for a compensation system that rewards merit, work to change these rules by demonstrating the value of quality service. If local policies, politics, or

---

2. Ron Zemke with Dick Schaaf, *The Service Edge: 101 Companies That Profit from Customer Care* (New York: New American Library, 1989), 70.

poverty blocks every avenue of financial reward, heighten the intrinsic rewards. Create situations in which service-oriented staff have the chance to work with patrons or projects viewed as especially desirable. Helping a local celebrity, working on a high-profile project, or working closely with a small group of patrons can be an extremely fulfilling experience and can show an employee that his supervisor recognizes his strengths. Although many factors will be involved in the evaluation and reward process, you must try to avoid publicly rewarding an individual known as a service Grinch.

An employee recognition program that focuses upon service can provide another effective form of rewarding staff. Create a program if one doesn't exist. Use it to reward continuing excellence in service as demonstrated by the problem solvers known by patrons and staff alike as the ones to turn to when they want service. Create awards for individual staff who have used creative and heroic measures to resolve a service problem, create a new service, or go the extra mile for some particular patron. Publicize these awards and encourage staff to recommend candidates for them. Honor all nominees, and publicize the names, pictures, and accomplishments of the winners. Award the winners something that they will value, such as money or a personal holiday, and something that may be posted for others to see, such as their name on a plaque or a personalized mug. Announce the awards in a public setting, and encourage all staff to join in the celebration. Use whatever mechanisms are available to reward service.

Planning Aid

The type of awards and recognition that will be valued by your staff and the criteria for offering awards will vary from library to library. A recognition program may begin small and build as time and resources permit. To identify where your library is weakest in recognizing staff accomplishments, you might start with an inventory of your recognition efforts. Working with staff and managers, rank the library's performance using figure 4.

Figure 4. Do We Recognize Good Service?

	Never	Rarely	RANKINGS Occasionally	Often	Always
1. My supervisor praises me when I make a special effort to help a patron solve a problem.	1	2	3	4	5
2. I feel as if my supervisor wants me to rush my work: quantity seems more important than quality.	1	2	3	4	5
3. When I bend a policy to help a patron, I am praised if the supervisor likes my decision.	1	2	3	4	5
4. When I bend a policy to help a patron, I am criticized if the supervisor dislikes my decision.	1	2	3	4	5
5. Merit raises are directly tied to service excellence.	1	2	3	4	5
6. People who might be described as "patron champions" get promoted.	1	2	3	4	5
7. I learn about the service contributions of other staff at library meetings.	1	2	3	4	5
8. I learn about the service contributions of other staff through the staff newsletter.	1	2	3	4	5
9. I learn about the service contributions of other staff through our bulletin board.	1	2	3	4	5
10. My annual performance review includes comments on my service contributions.	1	2	3	4	5

CHAPTER ELEVEN

Completing the Circle

C HAPTER ONE ENCOURAGED managers to include their staff and patrons in discussions to determine the library's mission. After focusing on mission identification, information gathering, planning, hiring, and training, it is time once again to return to your primary source for information about the library's performance. To evaluate your library, you must once again draw on input from staff and patrons.

Measuring What Is Important

The first step in measuring service is determining what to measure. Measurement takes time, so make sure that you focus on measuring services and activities that are important. It is amazing how many statistics are kept for no good reason while key indexes of service go unmeasured.

Administrators and funders often request the basic statistics charting the library's growth and use. As you determine what this group requires, develop more-focused reports that highlight the cost effectiveness of the programs or services that are measured.

Staff often favor statistics that document their growing work loads. Even if you don't need these statistics for any official reports, use them to spotlight staff accomplishments. Production statistics offer an easy opportunity to boast about current achievements and encourage even higher output.

Statistics that measure what is important to your patrons are the most crucial and challenging. Patron surveys, informally collected comments or criticisms, measures documenting library usage, and staff observations can alert you to those statistical areas that best reflect service impact on patron satisfaction.

Defining Performance Goals

Following is a list of specific service objectives that are important to library patrons.

convenient hours

appropriate books/journals

easy-to-find materials

adequate space for studying/reading

prompt service

friendly and knowledgeable staff

reliable and adequate equipment

simplicity of forms used to obtain service

In setting your library's standards for these or similar objectives, ask first what your patrons would describe as desirable. Listen carefully to patron definitions of quality service. Their views may differ from yours, ALA's, or the accrediting agency's. For instance, your patrons may prefer longer building hours and less service while you favor providing extended service during the current building hours. Junior-high students may request more group study areas while library association standards recommend individual study carrels.

Although limited time, space, and money force tough choices, use your patrons' perceptions to guide your decisions. *Servqual: A Multiple-Item Scale for Measuring Customer Perceptions of Service Quality*, describes a method for measuring the difference between customers' service expectations and their perceptions of the service. The authors recommend examining this difference to measure satisfaction. Superior service results not from meeting some formal standards, but from exceeding your patrons' expectations.[1]

Gathering Data

Measuring how your library is performing in the areas that your patrons value most requires statistical data, broad surveys, and personalized approaches. Statistical studies, described in Paul Kantor's *Objective Performance Measures for Academic and Research Libraries* and in the ALA publication *Output Measures for Public Libraries,* document the performance of key service operations such as the time it takes to fill an average interlibrary loan request or for a patron to find an in-house book and to check it out. *Measuring Academic Library Performance: A Practical Approach* offers some excellent examples of surveys that measure user perception of success and satisfaction with specific services such as asking a reference question or returning a book.

Statistical studies and surveys can offer essential data for measuring the performance of a unit or library. Meaningful service evaluations, however, must include personal and reflective input. To learn what patrons really want, ask them and ask your frontline staff. Develop a series of approaches to encourage comments from your staff and your patrons. Be ready to accept suggestions in any form. Publicize liaison names, phone numbers, and office and e-mail addresses. Give someone on staff the role of customer service representative, and establish a well-advertised hotline for service complaints, questions, and suggestions. If your library is large, create liaison positions to meet with groups with special needs.

To encourage input, have comment forms available at all service desks. Labeled with phrases such as "Talk to US (User Services)" or "We accept tips," these forms can encourage patrons to comment on service at the very moment when they have something to say. Remind staff that they too may use these forms

---

1. A. Parasuraman, Valarie Zeithaml, and Leonard L. Berry, *Servqual: A Multiple-Item Scale for Measuring Customer Perceptions of Service Quality* (Cambridge, Mass.: Marketing Science Institute, 1986), 5.

or may comment directly to their supervisors. Use the techniques that helped you gather input for the mission statement, e.g., focus groups, issues boards, and individual interviews. When giving presentations to staff or to patrons, remind them that their criticism is always welcome.

Studying the Results and Acting on Them

Whether you are gathering routine statistics, using a seasonal survey, or merely responding to patron complaints, organize your patron data. Organizing comments in a simple database software program such as QED Information Science's PC File will enable you to sort these comments a number of interesting ways. An academic library might sort responses by patron type (faculty, graduate student, administrator, undergraduate, external user, disabled student, etc.), college or department, branch library, service or function, specific patron concerns, and rank-ordered patron concerns. Whatever sorting method you select, thoughtful analysis of the list of patron comments should enable you to create a summary list of themes for review and planning. Major themes might include such concepts as the need to develop a program to deal with latchkey children, to improve retrieval of foreign patents and technical reports, or to heighten publicity alerting patrons to the higher fines for overdue videotapes.

No matter how you gather patron and staff suggestions, be certain to follow up on them. Thank the individual for the input, and convey the library's response. When a change is made based on a suggestion, highlight this fact. Show your staff and your patrons that the library really is listening and does implement change.

Planning Aid

Gather all of your patron complaints, suggestions, and compliments from the last year. Add staff suggestions and your own observations about patron satisfaction and concerns. Review these notes for recurring themes or patterns. Record them in broad categories, such as hours, general services, special services, staff attitude, staff knowledge and ability, building and space issues, instruction, collections, equipment, etc. The number and description of these categories will vary from library to library and department to department. Use this record of patron input to review recent annual reports and budget requests and to prepare future reports and requests. Ask yourself the following questions:

- Do the statistics, goals, and priorities reflect your patrons' expectations?
- Are the services and concerns of interest to your patrons highlighted in your reports?
- Are patrons routinely complaining about some area that is not addressed by your reports or budget planning?
- Is there any indication that patrons have noticed any service improvement you have fostered during the last year?
- Are you and your staff spending significant amounts of time on tasks that are of special interest to your patrons?

Keeping the Commitment

ERVICE IS AN "IN" TOPIC in America at this time. For libraries, however, service cannot be merely a passing interest. A library manager who hires staff to serve, orients them toward service, and arouses patron demand for service cannot abandon this commitment to follow a new fad. To develop a service-oriented organization, the top administration must make a long-term commitment to this ideal. In the vocabulary of the total quality management movement, this ongoing commitment requires a paradigm shift.[1]

Throughout the entire organization individuals must adopt a new way of looking at themselves and at their work. They must see themselves as part of an organization that is focused on customer needs and is committed to continuing improvement. In such an organization, staff training is part of daily life. Managers and staff should see change and growth as an expected part of their development. To master and promote new technologies and resources and to understand changing patron needs, staff at all levels must keep learning and growing. In good economic times

1. Stephen R. Covey and Keith A. Gulledge, "Principle-Centered Leadership: Mission, Vision, and Quality within Organizations," *The Journal for Quality and Participation* 15 (July/Aug. 1992): 70–78.

levels must keep learning and growing. In good economic times and in bad, the library manager must keep her commitment to training if the library is to keep its commitment to service.

Sample Mission Statements

Market Facts is a quality-directed marketing information company. Our core business is the performance of custom market research services. We are committed to growth and achieving leadership positions in the markets we have chosen.

It is the continuing mission of Market Facts to be a valued and reliable partner to our clients, employees, and shareholders.

- To our clients, we will provide quality products and services of genuine value that are responsive to their needs.
- To our employees, we will provide a challenging environment with the opportunity for personal growth.
- To our shareholders, we will strive to provide a fair and reasonable profit, recognizing our role as a responsible steward of their investment.

Our commitment to this vision will strengthen our market position and create an environment in which our clients, employees, and shareholders can prosper.

Courtesy of Market Facts, Arlington Heights, Ill.

It is the mission of Carpenter Technology to satisfy the specialty metal needs of our customers 100% of the time through excellence in the manufacture, marketing, and distribution of quality products. Through continuous improvement in everything we do, we will maintain a leadership position with our customers, treat our employees fairly, promote the integrity of the environment, retain the highest levels of ethical business conduct, and earn a competitive return on investment for our shareholders.

Courtesy of Carpenter Technology Corp., Reading, Pa.

To provide high quality services and collections to meet the needs of MIT's education and research programs. To provide a place conducive to discovery and self-education outside the classroom and laboratory. To share with the scholarly world at large the unique information resources of the MIT Libraries. To take an active role in the cooperative efforts that ensure access to and preservation of information resources for scholarly research.

Courtesy of Massachusetts Institute of Technology Libraries, Cambridge, Mass.

At Mead, our growth and success as a business enterprise depend on how well we satisfy our customers. Therefore, our goal is:

TO BE NUMBER ONE IN CUSTOMER SATISFACTION IN THE MARKET WE CHOOSE TO SERVE.

In achieving this goal, we will:

interact with our customers to understand their requirement and provide superior value by meeting or exceeding these expectations;

value the contributions of all employees and provide an environment in which each of us can contribute to the full extent of our talents and aspirations;

act, at every level in our company, to generate superior returns for share owners over the long term;

treat our suppliers as essential contributors to our success;

serve the communities in which we operate by performing successfully as a business enterprise and by being a responsible citizen.

At all times, our conduct will be guided by the ethical standards expressed by George H. Mead: "It is only by dealing honestly and fairly in all things that real success is attainable."

Courtesy of Mead Corp., Dayton, Ohio

Bibliography

Albrecht, Karl, and Ron Zemke. *Service America! Doing Business in the New Economy.* Homewood, Ill.: Dow Jones-Irwin, 1985.

American Management Association. *Close to the Customer.* New York: AMA, 1987.

Bureau of Better Business Practice. *BBP Customer Service Management Handbook.* Waterford, Conn.: Prentice-Hall, 1987.

Cannie, Joan Koob, with Donald Caplin. *Keeping Customers for Life.* New York: American Management Association, 1991.

Carr, Clay. *Frontline Customer Service: 15 Keys to Customer Satisfaction.* New York: John Wiley & Sons, 1990.

Carter, Joel. *Exceptional Customer Service.* Workshop offered by Dun & Bradstreet. South Bend, Ind., Dec. 1991.

Cottle, David W. *Client-Centered Service: How to Keep Them Coming Back for More.* New York: John Wiley & Sons, 1990.

Covey, Stephen R., and Keith A. Gulledge. "Principle-Centered Leadership: Mission, Vision, and Quality within Organizations." *The Journal for Quality and Participation* 15 (July/Aug. 1992): 70–78.

Kantor, Paul. *Objective Performance Measures for Academic and Research Libraries.* Washington, D.C.: Association of Research Libraries, 1984.

Kaul, Pamela A. "First Impressions Last (Effective Orientation Programs)." *Association Management* 41 (May 1989): 18, 29–31.

Lange, Arthur J., and Patricia Jakubowski. *Responsible Assertive Behavior: Cognitive/Behavioral Procedures for Trainers.* Champaign, Ill.: Research Press, 1976.

Liswood, Laura A. *Serving Them Right: Innovative and Powerful Customer Retention Strategies.* New York: Harper and Row, 1990.

Miller, Robert C. "Working in the Libraries." Notre Dame, Ind.: University Libraries of Notre Dame, 1990. Unpublished paper.

Myers, Pennie. *The Upset Book: A Guide for Dealing with Upset People.* Notre Dame, Ind.: Academic Publications, 1986.

National Institute of Business Management. *Service and Satisfaction: A Frontline Employee's Workbook.* New York: NIBM, 1989.

Parasuraman, A., Valarie Zeithaml, and Leonard L. Berry. *Servqual: A Multiple-Item Scale for Measuring Customer Perceptions of Service Quality.* Cambridge, Mass.: Marketing Science Institute, 1986.

Peters, Thomas J., and Robert H. Waterman, Jr. *In Search of Excellence.* New York: Warner Books, 1982.

Prytherch, Ray. *Handbook of Library Training Practice.* 2 v. London: Gower Publishing, 1986–1990.

Telephone Doctor Video Training Series. St. Louis, Mo.: The Telephone Doctor, 1983– .

Van House, Nancy, and others. *Output Measures for Public Libraries: A Manual on Standardization Procedures.* 2d ed. Chicago: American Library Association, 1987.

Van House, Nancy A., Beth T. Weil, and Charles McClure. *Measuring Academic Library Performance: A Practical Approach.* Chicago: The Association of College and Research Libraries, 1990.

Yates, Rochelle. *A Librarian's Guide to Telephone Reference Service.* Hamden, Conn.: Library Professional Publications, 1986.

Zemke, Ron. "Training in Campaign '92." *Training* 29 (Oct. 1992): 67–72.

Zemke, Ron, with Dick Schaaf. *The Service Edge: 101 Companies That Profit from Customer Care.* New York: New American Library, 1989.

Index

Assistant director for user services at the university of Notre Dame, Joanne Bessler believes in patron-focused libraries. Her publications "Do Library Patrons Know What's Good for Them" in the May 1990 issue of *Journals of Academic Librarianship* and "To Serve or Instruct—That Is the Question," a debate on the mission of the academic library at the 20th Annual Workshop on Library Instruction at Concordia University, Montreal, May 24, 1991, encouraged librarians to focus on their patrons' perceptions of their own needs.